THE GHOSTS OF BABYLON
Jonathan Baxter

Blackside Publishing
Colorado Springs, CO

Copyright © 2016 Blackside Publishing

All rights reserved. No portion of this book may be reproduced, distributed, stored in a retrieval system, or transmitted in any form or by any means, including photocopying, recording, or other electronic or mechanical methods, without the prior written permission of the publisher, except for brief quotations embodied in printed reviews and certain other noncommercial uses permitted by copyright law.

The Scripture quotation marked KJV is from the Holy Bible, King James Version (Authorized Version). First published in 1611. Quoted from the KJV Classic Reference Bible, Copyright © 1983 by The Zondervan Corporation.

For permission requests, email the publisher, addressed "Attention: Permissions Coordinator," blacksidepublishing@gmail.com

URL: www.blacksidepublishing.com

Ordering Information: Quantity sales. Special discounts are available on quantity purchases by corporations, associations, and others. For details, email: blacksidepublishing@gmail.com

Cover and book design by: Scoti Domeij

Printed in the United States of America

The Ghosts of Babylon/Jonathan Baxter

LCCN: 2016950482

ISBN 13: 978-1-68355-006-8, ISBN 11: 1-68355-006-4

First Edition

CONTENTS

Part 1: Back to Babylon

Back to Babylon 9
Al Anbar Nights 15
Jacking Off in the Port-O-John 18
Fourth of July, Fort Benning, Pre-Deployment 20
Cannelure 22
The Assaulters 24
The Death of a Ranger 31
When That Was Your War 34
Ghosts of the Khyber 37
Theories of Relativity 42
The Night the Giant Robots Came 44
The Jester Skull 46
Ghost Halls 53
A Love Like a War Zone 56
//NOTHING FOLLOWS 59
Moving Out, Moving On 62
Racetracks 64

Part 2: Mercenary Days

Love Notes to Ishtar in the Land of Two Rivers 73
A Thousand and One Nights 77
Ambien 80
Pilgrims 84

Tigris	87
The Thieves of Baghdad	89
Eid-al-Fitr, Baghdad, 2013	92
Event Horizon	94
My Box	98
Church	101
Another Love Song	103
These People	106
Of Electricity and Other Mysteries	110
Bearing Witness	114
The Enemy	117

*The bonds. The brotherhood.
The amalgam mash of oil and flesh.
An existence existing in a single breath
In a time we never fully understood.
The bonds. The brotherhood.*

—Leo Jenkins

For Ricky, Ryan, Pedro, Hannibal, Jankie, Kristoffer, Bobby and all the other Airborne Rangers in the Sky

FOREWORD

It takes from us innocence, and delivers an unparalleled view of the world in which we drift. It defines us, rapes us, builds us into pillars, and depletes the compassion hiding within our marrow.

A harsh and bleak understanding of the nature of man sits somehow symbiotically with the divine sanguinity of a life's spark, unwilling to extinguish. An evening of experiences takes a lifetime to absorb and an eternity to comprehend. A proving ground where generations of enthusiastic adolescents learn more about themselves in a day than can be achieved by any other decade's endeavor.

For those who have lived it, truly and completely lived it, war is reality. All else is but a shade of grey in its blinding technicolor. Nothing tastes the way fruit tastes after battle. Following an evening you knew you would not survive, nothing smells as good as the desert rain disrupting the parched arid landscape as the sun rises over the Euphrates.

Call it a gift if you will. Only a rare few among us possess it, the ability to stand in the fire of that crucible and walk away with something more to give. Even more seldom is one of those few capable of so accurately capturing the true and honest essence of man's bloodiest pastime.

The warrior poet is an endangered species. One that should be revered, for no academic, regardless how seasoned, will ever convey the essence of war better. No scholar has the capacity to duplicate the nuances splattered in bright red upon these pages. Poignant history told in fluid motion. The ink dances on paper like a stripper on stage, and in the true nature of the subject, nothing is held back.

I give my utmost respect and steadfast salute to Jonathan Baxter for the work which follows. *The Ghosts of Babylon* is as close to the fight as you can be without wearing armor.

There is a certain standard to which Rangers have always adhered. 100% and then some. Nothing less will ever do. Anyone who has ever lived by that standard, who has donned the coveted Ranger beret and scroll will feel the force of the work that follows. Any who have not, will become acutely aware of the sound a warrior's heartbeat makes.

Leo Jenkins
Former Army Ranger Medic

PREFACE

This poetry anthology is based on some of my experiences in Iraq and Afghanistan, first as a U.S. Army Ranger, and later as a private security contractor.

After my third deployment I started writing these poems and continued over the course of six years and nine more military and civilian deployments.

I was, at best, only an average member of my community. Compared to the others with whom I was privileged to work, my experiences were also just average, and simply my own. These poems attempt to articulate my memories and their frequently contradictory natures, including all the exhilaration, monotony, ugliness, and occasional beauty.

I wrote these for myself alone. My intent was to be as honest as possible with myself in the writing. To the end that I attained that honesty, I will consider this book a success. If others can look in and see some of their experiences and emotions reflected, I will consider this book that much more successful.

ACKNOWLEDGEMENTS

This publication would not have been possible were it not for the vision of Marty Skovlund, Jr. who created Blackside Concepts with the intent of providing a forum to America's veteran community. Blackside Concepts' offshoots—Blackside Publishing and *HavokJournal*.com—provided just such a forum, bringing together veterans from across the spectrum of this nation's conflicts to collectively share, purge and heal. While the government's various bureaucratic institutions struggle to address the many veterans' issues facing our country today, veteran-run enterprises come the closest to providing real support to our community. I am proud to be associated with Blackside Publishing and hope to watch this generation of veteran writers continue to come forward to share their unique, diverse experiences.

I would like to thank Gold Star Mother Scoti Domeij for her tireless work in putting together this book's layout and design. Her publishing experience guided this book to print, and I'm very grateful for her efforts.

I would like to thank the bibulous, peripatetic life-philosopher Leo Jenkins for taking time from his busy nomadic schedule to write the foreword of this book. I am a big fan of Mr. Jenkins' writing and his superlative story-telling abilities. I look forward to many future books from this most singular, literary adventurer.

I would like to thank my Marine father for introducing me to the Great Authors at an early age and teaching me that a warrior lifestyle is not incompatible with a literary one.

Lastly, I would be remiss not to recognize my wife, who continues to tolerate my many deployments, the ones to foreign lands and the ones to the more remote, interior places.

INTRODUCTION

Like the ancient Greek warrior-poet, Archilochus, Jonathan has walked the warpath and lived a life succumbing to the most primal of human endeavors. He's spent days best characterized by kill or be killed and losing friends in battle along with other monotonous experiences of war that aren't often talked about. I believe Jonathan, like Archilochus, will be remembered as someone who was as proficient with a pen as he was with the sword. He writes about emotionally complex subjects that are often hard to explain in simple terms. As you read his words you'll gain an elegant understanding of complex subjects that only come from the hands of a talented poet. What Jonathan records in *The Ghosts of Babylon* will be of paramount importance to anyone with an appreciation for posterity. History books yet to be written about the war on terror will rely on these verses.

As a fellow Ranger, I have an immense amount of respect for Jonathan. I know the depths of his intestinal fortitude and the near limitless amount of talent to accomplish what Jonathan has done—both in and out of uniform. As hard as it is to live the life of a Ranger, it's even more difficult to be a successful poet. Jonathan has performed at the pinnacle of war fighting, and I believe *The Ghosts of Babylon* is proof positive he's now performing at the pinnacle of writing poetry.

I hope you'll appreciate the following verses as much as I do. You'll be hard pressed to find another contemporary warrior-poet as talented as Jonathan. You'll be hard pressed to find another glimpse into the life of a warrior so emotionally raw as Jonathan's poetry. Take these words in and appreciate the blood, sweat, and tears that went into creating them. I know I do.

Rangers Lead The Way,
Marty Skovlund, Jr.

BACK TO BABYLON

PART 1

BACK TO BABYLON

"When the heavens above were yet unnamed
And the name of the earth beneath had not been recorded,
Apsu, the oldest of beings, their progenitor,
Mummu Tiamat, who bare each and all of them--
Their waters were merged into a single mass.
A field had not been measured, a marsh had not been searched out
When of the gods, none was shining,
A name had not been recorded, a fate had not been fixed . . ."
—*Enuma Elis, First Tablet*
Mesopotamia, circa 2nd Millennium BC
Budge Translation

Back to Babylon

The night is deep and warm and black
Our bus pulls slowly across the tarmac
The C-17 sits on the limitless track
Preparing to depart

There are no crowds, speeches or parades
But we wouldn't have it any other way
Just a quiet departure at the end of the day
When we fly into the night so long

The flight into the night that is endlessly long
Tonight we fly to Babylon

Back again to those nights under the thousand and one stars
Stars as bright as the eyes of Ishtar
Like white drops from a giant scimitar
That has cleft the green-black sky

I sling my pack and M4
Moving slowly towards that metal door
Back to where I was before
Back to the dawn of time

The engines emit a humming whine
We circle around the jet turbines
And in a file we shuffle and silently climb
Onto the waiting bird

Not a word is spoken as we climb aboard
Everyone lost in their own private world
The jet races down the track and into the sky is hurled
And we are gone into the night

Moving on towards the early morn
Ahead so many tasks for us to perform
A silent ship of souls we are carefully borne
On to the impending dawn

The dawn that dawned for countless years
Over an antique land of prophets and seers
Beyond our lowering ramp it will appear
In the pink and reddening dawn

The dawn of the days that are so hot and so long
The dawn of days in Babylon

Everyone is sprawled on the floor in a heap
Lost in their own drug-induced sleep
I can't read or rest or think of anything deep
As we fly across the sea

I've lost all conception of time and space
Moving along in some mindless race
Back to the ancient and ancestral place
Back to the land of two rivers

Back again to those historic places
The land of sand and green oases
Working again in the dark and twilight spaces
And we fly towards the dawn

Toward that dawn we're moving on
Moving on to Babylon

Back to those nights so sultry and warm
That bore us like riders on a mechanical storm
Green lasers and shadows like shape-shifting forms
Through the nights that were so black

Those nights that were black as the eyes of an eidolon
Those nights of nights in Babylon

I'm alone in a ship with a hundred men
My thoughts are here, then there, and now and then
Wondering who, and how, and if, and when
I'll have someone to tell me goodbye

The ramp will open and the smell will flood over us
That smell of sewage, burning trash, and dust
There to greet us as we descend to the waiting bus
There to welcome us home

Home again to the river's eternal shore
The land of gods, kings, heroes, and whores
We won't look back when we pass through this golden door
Beyond the far horizon

That lies like a prize beyond the far horizon
Here in the gardens of Babylon

Everyone is sore from the night on the floor
We walk stiffly from the bird's metal door
And we wander like survivors on the Ninevehan shore
Who have been cast from a great Leviathan

Like survivors cast from a great Leviathan
Here onto the shores of Babylon

Lying on my bed inside that great concrete fence
Riding out those nights of aching emptiness
In my music my heart beating that same cadence
It will all be over before long

Everything will end before very long
Just like the glory of Babylon

Here I am for the next hundred days
On to wherever my destiny lays
Cloaked in the sun's blinding rays
And the cold white embrace of the moon

The moon that shines over the *Nahr al-Furat*
Weaving its way from the slopes of Ararat
Through this land of palaces, hovels and ziggurats
As it has for the past thousands of years

And beneath its waters so murky and deep
So many secrets it surely must keep
The centuries of sediments have buried them heaped
In the banks of this ancient river

It's long past midnight and I'm high over the ocean
Floating on waves of my own emotions
Would that there were someone to receive my devotions
Well, maybe some other time

For now, I'll just sit here feeling this song
Feelings so full, they can't be wrong
The hum of the engines is steady and strong
As they carry me ever on

On and on and on and on
Taking me back to Babylon

> "My mother, during my night
> I became strong and moved about
> among the heroes;
> And from the starry heaven
> A meteor . . . fell upon me. . ."
> —The Epic of Gilgamesh
> Pennsylvania Tablet
> Mesopotamia, circa 2000 BC
> Jastrow and Clay Translation

Quick Reaction Force: A contingency element, fully kitted-up and ready to launch immediately in support of another element out conducting the actual mission. In other words: a long, long night waiting by the airfield . . .

Al Anbar Nights

Evening in Al Anbar

and the light of the moon impacts
on the tarmac where the Blackhawk sits
    rotors drooping low

the bulky shadows of the armored men prostrate
on the concrete are hard in their exoskeletons
    like so many dead beetles

trying to catch some heat
underneath the exhaust ports
of the bird trying to sleep
    another night on QRF

flat on my back
helmeted, my head
is upward to the night sky
      the cold stars are clear the desert air

white on green on black
through my NODs, the stars
      there are thousands

and the oceans of nebulae like
milk drops, glimpses from the past, suspended
in time are freeze-frames
      fast forwarded to us

and the stars, the suns
of systems, they are galaxies of worlds
      lifetimes of light years from here

here on this lunar landing pad
somewhere in the desert of some
    dusty moon that is Iraq

we are sojourners to antiquity, time
travelers back to the past as the
past travels back to us
    in the green-black sky

vectors of the past, collisions
of space-time suspended
    hanging above us

as we lie together on this pad
and try to keep warm by the exhaust vent
waiting out this ancient night

On this evening in Anbar

Jacking Off in the Port-O-John

> *"In Xanadu did Kubla Khan*
> *A stately pleasure-dome decree . . ."*
> —Samuel Taylor Coleridge, "Kubla Khan"

stale and putrid is the closet
rank and piled with specimen deposits
plastic heat compressed, closed in
alone at last my thoughts begin

outside the sands the winds disarray
hot breezes through my brain also play
mirrors cracking, fragment, explode
my dream begins, my surroundings erode

the tiny closet is replaced
as I step out of time and space
another world unfolds in my brain
a fantastic cityscape across a vast domain

replete with towers, cupolas, and minarets
chambers, halls, and battlements
and a stately pleasure dome I decree
is erected aloft over these empty seas

lotion cold-wet pours in my hand
taking up I start again
to paint my palace I resume
evoking the images of each room

naked figures I display
up and down my tapestry
that adorns the chambers in my mind
up and down the hallways entwined

with images full and warm appear
pulsing with life I do conjure
porn stars, old girlfriends, I gather them all
to come to life in my dream hall

my thoughts swirl and the images eddy
they dance about, the rhythm steady

and
GOD
i'm
LAUNCHED
in
TO
the
SKY

above the sand
the dust, the flies

coming back now
I'm sinking down

the walls close in
the smells abound

torn strips of paper on the floor
clips of fuck mags I've seen before
dried stains, old smells, the walls know years
of fear and grief and sand and tears

gone are the arches, the stairways, the towers
the halls, the chambers, the mirrors, the bowers
my blueprints, diagrams, and plans all discarded
in the blue water, crumpled, and I've departed

Fourth of July, Fort Benning Pre-Deployment

> *"Our revels now are ended. These . . . .*
> *were all spirits and*
> *Are melted into air, into thin air,*
> *And, like the baseless fabric of this vision,*
> *The cloud-capped towers, the gorgeous palaces,*
> *The solemn temples, the great globe itself,*
> *. . . shall dissolve,*
> *And, like this insubstantial pageant faded,*
> *Leave not a rack behind."*
> —William Shakespeare, *The Tempest*

fireflowers, blossoming, red-orange orchids
spiraling, pin wheeling, blue-green crocus

angels, weeping, electric tears from heaven
pyrotechnic pansies, fallen from the garden

red-green, circling, Chinese dragons
sailing neon seas on Spanish galleons

pop-pop-popping, bursting, a blooming
iridescence
smoke trails, hanging, a lingering
presence

pop-pop-popping, the fireworks exist and are
gone
brilliantly brief, but their memory lives
on

pop-pop-popping, the moment is achingly
here
forever in an instant, only to
disappear

but hanging behind in the dancing
phosphorescence
on the back of your eyelids, a momentary
essence

or drifting on the smoke that is fleetingly
near
then gone in a moment like a vanishing
tear

Cannelure

". . . we defy augury: there's a special providence in the fall of a sparrow. If it be now, 'tis not to come: if it be not to come, it will be now: if it be not now, yet it will come: the readiness is all."
—William Shakespeare, *Hamlet*

cannelure
kind of a peculiar word:
the groove of a projectile

such as a bullet

etched around the rifle round
keeping it sound in its place
secure in its casing

then winding like a toothy smile
as it describes the spiral of that round
revolving over the ground

reaching across those vast and intimate distances

cracking and resounding starts of sound
as the air is stretched and
snapped
like the fibers of some stringed instrument
played by some virtuosic maestro

and how the notes go
soaring, piercing, penetrating
projections of power across
the panoramas of the vistas
that we so violently occupy

beauty in lethality

like the writhing rainbow of some rock snake
or the silent gaze of some predatory shape
lurking in the deep
the arc of an Asian dagger
the stalk of a jungle panther

the Blackhawk formation racing through the night
the assaulters alighting
their lasers seeking, then finding
the darkness biding

the round spiraling through the night
as we revolve in this our flight
on our earth around our sun
in this course through time and space
orbits within orbits
millions of particles
racing and colliding
in crescendos of harmony and violence
a symphony of dissonance
distilled into the spiral of an alloy round
burning a tracer comet trail
describing a journey
a narrative arcing toward an ending
a metal messenger winding its way
to whatever home it may find
in bone or flesh or rock or desert earth

The Assaulters

"We few, we happy few . . ."
—William Shakespeare, *Henry V*

The OPTEMPO was pretty high in cities like Ramadi prior to the 2007 Al Anbar Awakening. Many of our missions were against Time Sensitive Targets. Our platoon would stage our Stryker vehicles in an old graveyard out in the city and loiter, waiting for the launch command.

> the assaulters lounge
> sprawled languidly in the oppressive heat
> like so many hunting dogs
>
>
> on the Stryker's ramp
> relaxed, our heads back against the door frame
> muscles charged with latent energy
>
>
> leaning back in our kits
> we sit, helmets off, radio traffic
> idly crackles in the background
>
>
> waiting on THE WORD

rifle muzzles down
hands contouring down lower receivers
fingers curved over triggers

the metal ramp is littered
bottles filled with dip spit collect
like the sunflower seeds at our boots

we're territorial like that

the conversations flow
the profanity spoken like poetry
pungent punctuation marks

pop pop pop
dip can coming out of shoulder pocket
communion plate passed around

the raunchiest stories ever
war obscenities, sexual outrages
the funniest stories you ever heard

outbursts of laughter
like the dip spit spilling out from our lips
"you cannot make up this shit!"

walk away from the group
to piss by the tombstones, return again
to resume staining the dust with spit

and the laughter is
an affirmation, group absolution
more sacred than could come from a priest

*"I get it, dude. That's fucked up, and you're fucked up,
but I get it because I'm fucked up too."*

and you'll never be alone
so long as we're here with you
on this Stryker ramp
here in this graveyard
somewhere in Babylon

and like that the moment is passed
as the WORD descends like the Hand of God
Launch or RTB

we put our MICHs on
and cram back into our metal cocoons
never to return to that moment

it briefly hangs behind us
over the sunflower seeds and dust stains
before slowly fading away

some of us move on
we make some attempts to remain in touch
but it will never be the same

not like it was back then

some of us try to settle
into the REAL WORLD, where we try to speak
a new language unstained by tobacco

or dead baby jokes
where civilians measure your cock by your
salary, car, or social status

and not by your competence
or by how well you shoot or by the
weights you can throw around in the gym

or that certain assurance
in your voice as you cross that last threshold
into that yawning and hungry darkness

lit only by your taclights

"Need one!"
"Got one!"
Touch.
Entry.
"Clear."
"Clear."

assimilating into
a world where the friendships are measured in
the affectations of affability

not in the burden of shared misery
Ft. Benning in the dark before the dawn
another platoon formation run

around the airfield
carrying forty pound water jugs then
buddy-carries up Cardiac Hill

the Legs look at us
furtively, like domestic animals
eyeing a wolfpack stealing by

halfway point
you carried me, now I will carry you
to the top of this damn hill

we assimilate
keeping lonely midnight vigils as we
make myths out of our memories

as we relive the past
looking at the photos, raising a glass
consecrated to those passed

and failing to adjust
going back to the closest thing we can find
wearing civvies this time

and slinging up our rifles
we go seeking the warrior culture
trying to find the past in the future

we return again
to the land we left where we try to find
that which we left behind back there

trying to find that moment again

but the only ones
who never truly left that moment were
the ones who joined with it forever

in an instant's flash
in the crushing overpressure or in
a single shot in a darkened room

or the ones who dived
into a substance-abuse death spiral
or health crisis or car crash

they left the moment
only to become one with it later
in another time and place

these are the only ones forever in the moment now

we drink to it
dream of joining it, give it labels like
Valhalla, Hall of the Slain

but it's back there
in that old, dusty Ramadi graveyard
the rooftops and the airfields

back there in the places
where we bided our time in the moments
that we shared and that defined us

The Death of a Ranger

*"The hero slain in battle—
Thou and I have often seen such a one—
His father and mother support his head,
and his wife [kneels] at his side.
Yea! The spirit of such a man is at rest."*
—*The Epic of Gilgamesh, Tablet XII
Mesopotamia, circa 2000 BC
Muss-Arnolt Translation*

So, you heard a Ranger died today
What a tragic waste, you said
That he should die in a foreign land
With so much of life ahead

He still had so much left to do
He was too young, you lament
Why should a man like him have to die
With so much of his life unspent?

Yes, it's true, he was too young
And his death is a tragedy
But don't you ever call it a waste
That is not for you to say

He was only in his twenties
While you're in the middle of life
But I tell you that he lived more
As a result of all this strife

For have you ever leapt out of a plane
In the darkest hour of night
Or rode a Blackhawk into a fight
With your legs hanging over the side?

Did you ever creep outside
The enemy's safe house at night
With all your senses burning like fire
Did you ever feel quite so alive?

Did you ever feel the rush of assault
Of kicking down doors in the dark
And clearing a house from bottom to top
Have you ever had feelings so stark?

Did you ever hear the crack
Of a rifle round overhead
And laugh aloud to your buddies around
Because it wasn't your time yet?

Did you ever weep at a brother's death
And have his blood red on your hands
And know what it's like to leave a part of yourself
Behind in some far foreign land?

Did you ever take the lessons you learned
And bring them back home to the States
And live the next months in a special way
"With a heart for any fate?"

Did you ever bike to the top
Of a forested mountain place
And ride to the bottom as fast as you could
With the wind bringing tears to your face?

Did you ever drink and joke and laugh
With a tugging wistfulness
And hold the memories of the times with your friends
And store them away just in case?

For just as one who's never been cold
Can ever truly know heat
And just as one who's never been hungry
Can ever truly taste what he eats

So you who have never known risk
Or danger or loss or fear
Can ever truly appreciate life
And hold every moment dear

So, yes, a Ranger died today
Join me in tears at his grave
But speak not about a wasted life
Or I'll make you eat every word you say

For, yes, a Ranger died today
And it's tragic his life should cease
But he lived more in his few years of war
Than you in your decades of peace

In memory of SGT William Patrick "Ricky" Rudd
  KIA October 5, 2008
  Operation Iraqi Freedom

When That Was Your War

"My friend, you would not tell with such high zest
To children ardent for some desperate glory,
The old Lie: Dulce et decorum est
Pro patria mori."
—Wilfred Owen
"Dulce et Decorum Est"

You fought through forests of Argonne
And choked on poison gas
You stormed the beaches of Peleliu
And on coral sands breathed your last

You beheld the coast of Normandy
And ran that fatal shore
You fought so well before you fell
When that was your war

You wrote your final letters
And left them in your trench
And then over the top and on to your fate
In a machine gun's fiery clench

You shook with malaria and typhus
In a thousand tropical climes
You died like the flies that clung at your eyes
To the mosquitoes' deadly whine

You tripped on the bodies of your brothers
As you walked through the smoke and the fire
And lay down before the God of War
Like offerings at a funeral pyre

You knew the far borders of horror and pain
And their darkest, most secret realms
You explored the corners of deepest Hell
And in its innermost rings you dwelled

And I sit, relaxed and serene
On a secure forward operating base
In my climate-controlled KBR unit
It is a most comfortable place

I have flat screen TVs with surround sound
A hard drive with a thousand movies
And a climate-controlled MWR room
Where I can call home whenever I please

Tonight I'll go to the gym and work out
Go to the chow hall and grab a plate
And later in my climate-controlled bathroom
I'll leisurely masturbate

They call me a hero back home
Though I haven't done anything brave
You gave all that you could and then some
And when you had nothing left, you gave

And it seems I have it so much better
Than the thousands who went before
But that was then and this is now
And now this is my war

And I guess blood smells the same in any place
In any time or war
And I guess his mom cried as hard as yours
When she heard that knock on the door

Cause Death keeps the pace and we all run this race
And though mine's a different course
He still keeps the score
In both this my war and yours

And though the struggles and conflicts are different
Than the ones that came before
The name of the game is still the same
And every generation will have its war

Ghosts of the Khyber

"When you're wounded and left on Afghanistan's plains."
—Rudyard Kipling
"The Young British Soldier"
Barrack-Room Ballads

Last night I had the strangest vision
As I lay asleep on my cot
I dreamed we were out on a mission
And I must have gotten lost

For I found myself alone on "a darkling plain"
Under a star-filled black green sky
I looked for the rest of my platoon in vain
They had vanished in the night

So I set out for the horizon line
Across that vast and rocky plain
And after awhile I began to climb
Into the foothills of a mountain range

And as I climbed higher
I felt the air getting lighter
And I climbed ever higher
Into the Khyber
Into the mountains of the Khyber Pass

And as I labored through the darkness
I saw a light gleaming bright through my NODs
I could see it beneath a rocky escarpment
And moving figures, as through a fog

I worked my way closer to this light
And was surprised to find there
A well-established bivouac-site
And in the center, a roaring fire

And there beside the leaping flames
Three figures were reclined
They laughed and joked without restrain
And drank from skins of wine

A more motley group I could not imagine
How they came together baffled me
They wore the trappings of infantrymen
But from different stages in history

The first had a weapon with a familiar profile
I picked him out first from the rest
By his side was a Kalashnikov rifle
And he wore fatigues and a load-bearing vest

The second wore a bright red jacket
And an ammo belt with leather straps
On his head was a white pith helmet
And he sported a striking mustache

The third of the three was the most unique
He had a circular shield and a long spear
He wore only sandals and a red tunic
His face had been worn by the years

And they sat by the fire
And the flames leapt up higher
And they drank by the fire
In the shadow of the Khyber
In the shadow of the Khyber Pass

They saw me standing, a bit removed
And called me over to the fireside
They bade me sit and eat their food
And offered me some wine

"Relax, comrade," said the first of the three
"From us you have nothing to fear
We've all been fighting the same enemy
And we're all on the same side here"

For he had launched raids against the same mujaheddin
As a member of the Soviet Spetsnaz
And done helo-borne raids just like me
And fought in the same valleys and draws

"At last," he said, "it came to an end
When our bird went down in a fiery crash
Just over there, around that bend
In the shadow of the Khyber Pass."

The mustached man had found a bottle of gin
At the bottom of his old rucksack
He flashed at me a knowing grin
As he tilted the bottle back

"It was here I also met my fate,"
He said after he finished his swig
"It was late in the year 1878
At the Battle of Ali Masjid"

"We were shoulder to shoulder, charging en-masse
I remember it vaguely, like a dream
As we stormed their fort at the top of the Pass
And I died a loyal soldier of the Queen"

"A tribesman's arrow was what did it for me,"
Said the third with the weathered face
"When I came through here in the fourth century BC
In the army of Alexander the Great"

We finished off the Macedonian's wine
And the Brit shared the rest of his gin
The Russian produced some vodka by and by
And we all commenced drinking again

And we sat by the fire
And the flames leapt up higher
And we drank by the fire
Me and the ghosts of the Khyber
The ghosts of the Khyber Pass

And we swapped war stories for hours on end
About the engagements, large and small
And we cursed the wretched Afghans
And wished death upon them all

At last the hills began to grow light
The morning chill hung damp in the air
The fire sputtered and clung to life
I could barely see the others there

I slowly got to my feet and stretched
"My friends, I must be getting on
Thank you for this most welcome rest
But I can see it's almost dawn"

The Macedonian looked up at me then
A gentle look on his rough-hewn face
"Just sit yourself down and rest, my son,
You've already become one with this place"

"Be at peace, my son, and don't be afraid
You're one with the thousands who have gone here before
And here with their memories will forever remain
In these hills that are older than war"

And at his words, I looked down at my hands
They were faint in the pale morning light
And I knew that now I would never leave these lands
That here my spirit would ever abide

So, I sat by the fire
With my brothers by the fire
And the smoke drifted higher
And we were one with the Khyber
Me and the ghosts of the Khyber
The ghosts of the Khyber Pass

Theories of Relativity

*"For there is nothing either good or bad,
but thinking makes it so . . ."*
—Shakespeare, Hamlet

You turn some switches off
And some switches on
Or maybe that's what I learned in Babylon

The reality is clear, you see?
It's all different theories of relativity

Everything is solely
What you choose to make it mean for you
Whatever you need to believe
You can make it all come true

That which is real is that which you feel
The rest are extrapolations
The religions, life teachings, and philosophies are
Simply spiritual masturbation

The pleasures and the pain
They're just transmissions in your brain
Once you accept that concept
You'll see the naked woman as only an object

As the man in the cave is just a target

The night assault, a scripted, yet improvisational play
And the gun's recoil feels like just another day at the range
The corpse in the ditch is just a pile of meat and hair
You just walk away and leave him lying there

That we call fear is just a physical response
A quickening of breath, an acceleration of pulse
An opening of pores and a release of sweat
Just like that we call love is only sex

The neurons firing in your mind
Adrenaline high
Dopamine high
These are how we get by

These are the only things that are truly real at all
The rest are merely shadows dancing on a cave wall

The Night the Giant Robots Came

*"Fundamentals of the raid include
- - Surprise and speed . . .
Violence of action."*
—*The U.S. Army Ranger Handbook*

The night the giant robots came
I lay awake in bed
They came across from the house next door
We heard them overhead

There was the loudest noise I ever heard
A boom and a shuddering crash
They pounded down the narrow stairs
And crunched on broken glass

I closed my eyes and covered my ears
And wished them all away
But they shouted orders I couldn't understand
And forced us to obey

They were big and tall and gray and black
Their eyes were glowing green
Bright lights shone from their heads and guns
I hoped I wouldn't be seen

They dragged my Daddy into the next room
They covered his head with a bag
My Mommy she shook and prayed and cried
And wiped my face with a rag

They searched our house up and down
There was the crash of a breaking plate
They waved a wand over my Mommy and me
Although I was only eight

The night the giant robots came
It seemed just like a dream
I kept drifting in and out of sleep
I remember just brief scenes

Me sitting on the tile floor
The robots searching each room
Their asking strange questions of my Mommy while I
Was hoping they all would leave soon

The morning after the robots left
Dawned like any other day
I woke up and yawned and looked around
My Mommy had nothing to say

She had tidied the rooms and swept the floors
There was no more sharp glass on the ground
But our door was black and twisted and bent
And my Daddy couldn't be found

For Maria

The Jester Skull

"As long as houses are built, as long as tablets are sealed,
as long as brothers are at enmity,
as long as there exist strife and hatred in the land,
as long as the river carries the waters [to the sea]
... the goddess of fate, she who ... determines fate, will do so,
... But the days of death are unknown to mankind."
—The Epic of Gilgamesh, Tablet X
Mesopotamia, circa 2000 BC
Muss-Arnolt Translation

Last night a vision came to me
A grinning, laughing skull
That hung above a bony frame
And was cloaked in a funeral pall

A brightly colored fool's cap
Was perched upon his brow
With colorful bangles all dangling
And on his shoulder sat a crow

His black cloak hung about
His bleached white shoulder blades
And a jewel-encrusted scepter
He jauntily displayed

All hail the Jester King!
The skull loudly exclaimed
All across these far lands
My orders are proclaimed

All persons high and lowly
With fortunes great and small
From the scholars to the ignorant
All must dance at the Jester's Ball

Hearken to my words, he said
As he laid his long fingers on my head
I'll tell you of strange things, he said
And fantastic visions of the dead

He lifted his sparkling scepter
And beat a rhythm on the ground
A fluty melody played through his ribs
My head began to pound

The mighty and the powerful
The skull, chuckling, said with glee
Must exchange their crowns for my jester's cap
And meekly dance for me

The richest of men I'll summon
Their jewels will turn to rust
Their treasures and moneys will crumble away
Dust compounded with dust

The most beautiful of maidens
Those paragons of form
Will wither away to dust with dismay
And host my legions of worms

Every girl's desires and fancies
Every boy's hopes and dares
Will be like dew on a summer's day
And vanish into the air

All the life works and legacies
Of every grandmother and father
Will simply swirl and ripple away
Like paintings in the water

All of the great works of art
The poems, paintings, and songs
Will disappear under my hourglass sands
And leave nothing but a desert of sound

So all that's beautiful in this world
I, wondering, mused out loud
Will all vanish away with time
And dissipate like clouds?

It all will be lost, I flatly said
As I looked at a wasteland of bones
All the hopes and dreams and fears
The loves and the longings all gone?

It will all have been for nothing
Nothing will remain of it all
When we all arrive to dance
To dance at the Grim Jester's Ball

The skull, he laughed and smiled
And flashed at me a grin
He beckoned me closer with a long white finger
And to my soul he peered in

Let me tell you a secret, his ancient voice hissed
I have secrets and secrets to spare
Beneath my cloak so many mysteries abound
That of this one I'll make you aware

Yes, you will die, and your beloved will die
And of you nothing will remain
Your monuments and testaments will all be made low
And crumbled to dust on this plain

But there are moments, brief moments and few
That shine like stars in the night overhead
They light the night with a crystalline light
Over this road to your destiny dread

And in those moments
Those stark naked moments
Those scintillations from the flame

You will be so
Incredibly alive
That from you I nothing can claim

In the still of the night
In the morning's first light
In the sound of the falling rain

In your lover's embrace
Or the wind in your face
Or the joy of a dream attained

So go and be free
And one day I'll see
You on this road one day
When, I won't say
But that will be the day
That you come to your home with me

So live while you can
And take every chance
And embrace the romance
Before forever you dance
Forever you dance with me

And he twirled his scepter
And swirled his robe
And turning he strode
Not for a moment he slowed
As he merrily walked down the road

I saw him once in the distance
So far that I could barely see
The light was glinting off his cap
He was looking back at me

So I'll meet him down the road some day
With all his gray-robed thralls
But for now I'll live for the moments of the day
Before I dance at the Jester's Ball

Ghost Halls

"No rays from the holy Heaven come down
On the long night-time of that town;
But light from out the lurid sea
Streams up the turrets silently—
Gleams up the pinnacles far and free—
Up domes—up spires—up kingly halls—
Up fanes—up Babylon-like walls . . ."
—Edgar Allan Poe
"The City in the Sea"

I walked the ghost halls and it was late
and hung with the ideals we have chosen to elevate
the stone altars and grave graven images
there in that shadow hall under the mirror ball

these things we have chosen to make holy
to dedicate, consecrate
tapestries and masterpieces
intertwined with their own lies
woven with the banality of our own lives

and over here, in this mausoleum of museums
the depiction of the Hero at War
doesn't the spirit soar?

and over his beauteous head
his battle flag stained in red

all the symbols and the colors
shining over all the others

how can there be any other?

and the lovers!
cloaked in marble
their love will never falter
never stale, never pale
or become mechanical and trite

just as our hero will never sway in his fight
never doubt his cause is right

or commit one possible injustice
as he metes out the justice
the righteous justice of his god

and lording over all
the most sacred image of them all

the Being wisest, most holy
seated in the infinite Trinity

with ideals such as these
who could ask for more?

a perfect love, a noble cause, a holy war
what a perfect allegory
for good and evil

and behold our Hero!

the champion in the strife
who would gladly give his life
for his cause most right

over and over again
these ideals, these idols
no room in these halls
for the sinners, the pariahs

the fighters who were neither heroes nor whose causes
were stainless . . .

the hall is shape-shifting and phantasmal
the walk liquescent and mercurial

watching the flowing tapestries
like so many water paintings
the hero is black, Caucasian
Crusader, Saracen

the god a wise patriarch
calligraphic brush stroke

Jehovah, Allah
fat, oriental idol grinning
dancing demon

the laws, canons, doctrine, dogmas
confetti-like, spewing words and laws

tower of Babel come crashing down
and the Sound!

here in the kaleidoscope hall
under the broken mirror ball

where the shadows seek their king and prostrate
make offerings as to a snake

and the phantom wanderers walk the empty ground
footfalls falling and seeking after a sound

A Love Like a War Zone

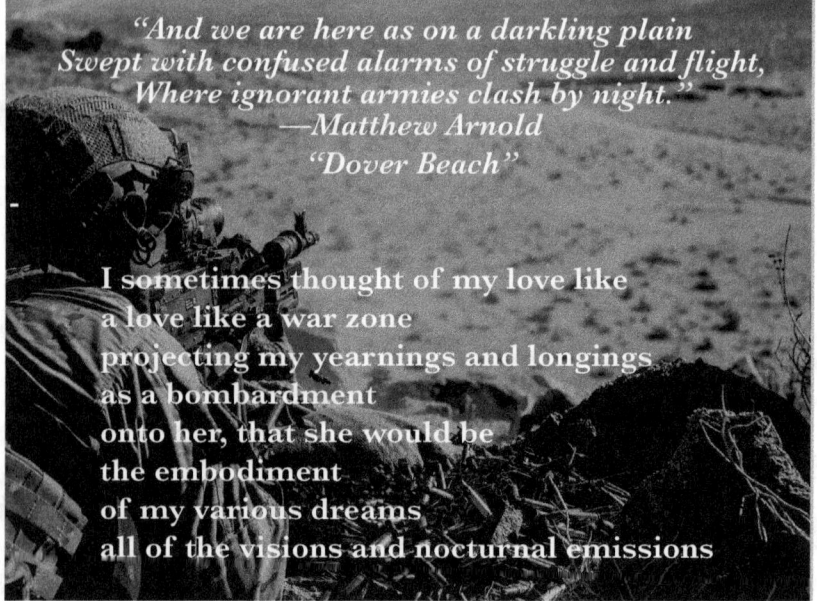

*"And we are here as on a darkling plain
Swept with confused alarms of struggle and flight,
Where ignorant armies clash by night."*
—Matthew Arnold
"Dover Beach"

I sometimes thought of my love like
a love like a war zone
projecting my yearnings and longings
as a bombardment
onto her, that she would be
the embodiment
of my various dreams
all of the visions and nocturnal emissions

And I could create these templates
of beauty and grace
and give them her face
just as I project all the rage and hate
and lead at the alien races
vie to erase whatever traces
of existence they possess
leave nothing left
but piles of shell casings and burning husks
as I take down these constructs
of all that I loathe and despise
as when I look in her eyes
I can surmise that she is to be
the one truly meant for me

Constructing my love
as I construct my enemy

And she will be the one to bear my song
and I can put it in words for her
some kind of verse

Or is that absurd?
because when I look at her
I don't really know her at all
just like I didn't know that Haj
but I was quick to laugh
when the ordnance erased him in a blast

He was my enemy
the object of my loathing
and disgust and he must
burn in the flames of that Hellfire strike
we were nothing alike
he didn't have dreams or plans for a better life

Maybe we never truly know ourselves in the end
just as we never truly know those with whom
we intersect in this life
violent intersections
skirmishes, firefights, kinetic strikes
nights of passion lighting up
like flares in the sky
neon flashes through a hotel window
firing the bed in freeze-frames
of red and green
as in the black and green
the white lasers dance over the target objective

like the lights on the dancers lit on the stage in front of me
flesh on display
or naked and flayed
in some post-blast battle damage assessment

My lover, do I know her
and my enemy, though he died screaming
did I ever really see him?

Just as I wonder if I can really make out myself
out there on point in body armor and Kevlar
seeing myself from afar
carbine at the high ready
IR floodlight on and scanning
through the mist and the gloaming
always searching, never knowing

So much love to give, so much life to feel
but it seems it's only in my dreams
on this my battlefield
searching for what is real

As I move out into the night
heading up that draw toward that ridge
trying to bridge that space between my mind and my life
climbing into the evening
where, gently, she receives me

Looking to the stars as I chart my way home
home and free from this my war zone

//NOTHING FOLLOWS

"I walk the secret way
With anger in my brain.
O music through my clay,
When will you sound again?"
—Siegfried Sassoon
"A Mystic as Soldier"

The DD-214: The "Holy Grail" of the out-processing quest, received upon separation. The discharge document that chronicles one's military career, schools, awards, deployments, and time in service.

> **11. PRIMARY SPECIALTY** (List number, title and years of specialty. List additional specialty numbers and titles involving periods of one or more years.)
> 11B2V 00 INFANTRYMAN - 5 YRS 9 MOS//NOTHING FOLLOWS
>
> **13. DECORATIONS, MEDALS, BADGES, CITATIONS AND CAM[PAIGN] RIBBONS AWARDED OR AUTHORIZED** (All periods of servic[e])
> AFGHANISTAN CAMPAIGN MEDAL W/ CAMPAIG[N]
> //IRAQ CAMPAIGN MEDAL W/THREE CAMPAIG[N]
> //JOINT SERVICE COMMENDATION MED[AL]
> [...]ON MEDAL//JOINT SERVI[CE]
> [...] ACHIEVEMENT AWAR[D]

I receive my DD-214 as a reprieve
from the fat black woman behind the desk
and place it with the rest of my papers I have gathered
that were scattered like Easter Eggs
hidden around Soldier's Plaza
in one blow-out extravaganza

The thick folder I hold here is my monument
to the acquisition of all my separation documents
Running in the rain through the street
hunting signatures like I once hunted HVTs
kicking down doors
blowing past bored civilian employees
chasing down that DD-214

And I got it. I'm done. Nothing Follows.

My DD-214 is pretty modest indeed
My six year career fits almost completely on one sheet
A few sentences spill over onto the second
bookended by: //NOTHING FOLLOWS

The six deployments fit into one box
a jumble of numbers, lines and dots
I sift through the dates
each recounting a different place in my life

That one was my first
That one there was the worst
We lost Ricky there
That one was my first to Afghanistan
the land where time began
That one was my favorite and
//NOTHING FOLLOWS

I hoist my giant folder
and make my way to the door and homeward

Clutching my beret, I head into the rain
trying to keep the papers dry inside my jacket
protecting the one and a quarter page testament
to whatever the past six years meant:

boredom, tedium, fear
anxiety, imposed celibacy
separation, sexual frustration

physical exhaustion, a few brief moments of fulfillment
those times you were God for a minute
and brotherhood

Tonight I'll get drunk and moody with some of my buddies
Pitch myself a little pity party

For now I get in my car and start driving to a new horizon

Here's the freedom that you dreamed of for the past few years
but why does the sky appear so empty now?

Empty like the second page of my discharge document
ending in that final and hollow statement:
//NOTHING FOLLOWS

Moving Out, Moving On

> "As I muse, retrospective, murmuring a chant in thought,
> Lo! the war resumes- again to my sense your shapes,
> And again the advance of armies."
> —Walt Whitman
> "Ashes of Soldiers"

and I still miss the sound of helicopters
sitting in the door, legs over the side
through the night, just living the ride

shoulder to shoulder with my brothers' armor
riding down the sky beneath the rotors' thunder

riding down the sky with you, my brother

and there was no night too dark for us then
no valley of the shadow too low for us to descend

like the wrath of some biomechanical god

when we were the vanguard of the storm
harbingers of the god of war

and witnesses to the awe

of those precision bombing runs
and the orgasmic bursts of the miniguns

looking up to watch the tracers slowly arc
ahead of the machine guns' steady bark

crossing the sky like a stream of red ejaculate

and beyond, twinkling in their mystery so high
the thousand stars against the green-black sky

shooting stars leisurely overhead
as you chased down some raghead

hot and sweaty in your exoskeleton

and already those memories are so distant to me now
like shadows somewhere far beyond tracer burnout
fading, and now gone
like the spent brass cartridge casings I left like those
parts of myself
on that ridge, that field, that draw

moving out, I'm walking point on a one-man patrol
onward to a place that maybe one day I'll know

alone and onward to the dawn
but I suppose life is all about moving on

the team I left behind is getting ready tonight
to go carry out dark acts in the black of night

putting on body armor and heading out to the birds
to try to find some bloody equilibrium in this world

and I'm just sitting at a white and black computer screen
writing out memories that were black and green

riding out another night to the dawn

and I'll always miss the sound of helicopters

Racetracks

"If you can wait and not be tired by waiting..."
—Rudyard Kipling
"If—"

The C-17 makes its midnight run
Inside the jumpers stand one by one

Like so many beasts of burden
swayed by the gentle turbulence

Going through the pre-jump checklist

Hook Up

HOOK UP

Part pantomime
part old-time chorus line

Check Static Lines

Lead and chorus, keeping time

CHECK STATIC LINES

As we go through our little song and dance skit

Check Equipment

Just waiting to get on with it

CHECK EQUIPMENT

Sound Off For Equipment Check

Okay

Okay

As I set patiently in traffic today

Okay

Okay

A thousand miles and as many years away

Okay

Okay

Waiting on the light to change from red to green

Okay

Okay

While across the way

Okay

Okay

The clashing masses claw and scream

Okay

Okay

For the best deals beneath the Christmas lights red and green

Okay

Okay

Tis only the season
to suspend all reason

ALL OKAY, JUMPMASTER

And then:

One Minute

Can't fill it

ONE MINUTE

We just can't fill it

No matter how much we consume

Thirty Seconds

It will never fill us

THIRTY SECONDS

We're left with only the remnants

Six Americans died last week
but the only news there seems to be

Drop zone coming up, standby

Is some reality star's new controversy

And without further notice
our pass is aborted

Countdown retracted
Adrenaline-drip protracted

The pilot settles into a leisurely orbit
We lean against our static lines and focus

On the weight of the harness
hanging like a hundred-pound carcass

And the discomfort turns to numbness

Racetracks around the DZ
waiting for the door light to turn from red to green

My life in a different holding pattern now it seems
waiting on the traffic light's decree

Racetracks transposed, I suppose

Orbiting between the house, the grocery store, the make-ups, the fights
All the great questions distilled down to
"what-are-we-having-for-dinner-tonight?"

Regulated by that goddamn traffic light

And to the west, the snow-covered Rockies stretch
like some other ranges from long ago

Horizons transposed, I suppose

You can take me away from the green and the black
but I'm locked into another racetrack

Choking on a silent scream
waiting on that light to turn from red to green

MERCENARY DAYS

PART 2

MERCENARY DAYS

"[And the goddess Ishtar said:]
'Come, Gilgamesh, be thou my spouse,
Give, O give unto me thy manly strength.
Be thou my husband, let me be thy wife,
and I will set thee in a chariot
[embossed] with precious stones and gold,
with wheels made of gold, and shafts of sapphires.'"
—The Epic of Gilgamesh, Tablet VI, Mesopotamia
circa 2000 BC, Muss-Arnolt Translation

Love Notes to Ishtar in the Land of Two Rivers

Ishtar: The Babylonian goddess of love and war. Unlike her Greek and Roman successors, Venus and Mars, Ares and Aphrodite, each of whom symbolized only one of these two attributes, Ishtar represented both of these opposing themes in one complex, alluring dichotomy . . .

and that fast I'm back
touchdown
home in Iraq
and it's like I never left her at all

maybe a part of me never did
innocent
the part that was still a kid
and I lost somewhere out in the desert

in ways it's like returning to an old lover
familiar
the old places to rediscover
the old experiences to relive

all the old memories creep back
soft
like the impending night attack
that steals over the evening fields like the dark

I'm replaying the old scenes
black and green
flashing across my mind's screen
like a shadow play viewed from afar

all those same smells are there
redolent
hanging in the night air
in the blanket that quilts the quiet, silent stars

following after your star
elusive
now I have come so far
come so far since Al Anbar

And circular is the road that brought me to this place
To you, goddess of love and war
Now I'm back at the golden door
In the land where once was your sacred gate

They worshipped you here in the ancient past
There are those of us who keep the faith still
And I'm just trying to feel as fulfilled
As that time I had you, once, at last

And maybe I'll never come that close again
But that's why we play this game
Hoping and praying to re-attain
That time when you and she were one and same

This the most seductive of games
You play it once, all else is tasteless
Calling you to seek after its traces
And you come, a moth to the flame

to touch at her, chase after her
glimpses
through the clouds of a star
and catch her scent that winds on the wind from the river

distant glimpses like the popping of
far off small arms
far off flashes
distant like heat lightning

And maybe that's the closest you'll be to her again
But still you follow on
After that siren's song
And maybe you would follow till the end

For that chance to be in her arms once more
To hear her voice sound in the rotors
Like the weapon recoiling into your shoulder
And the smoke like her hair curling from its bore

her hot in your blood
electric
the most addictive drug
the most seductive game you ever played

Like notes from a far off song
These memories are a dream
Maybe never again to be
Yet still I follow along

Bringing me back to this place
Counting the days, killing the time
Living it easy on the government's dime
As the days march by in a steady pace

watching the days drift by
ghost days
the sun stark in the sand's haze
hanging in the sky like a dead fish's eye

Patiently waiting for her promising night
A solitary temple guard
I can again watch for her star
And time stands still in the absence of light

And I will keep my watch until the dawn
Watching the lights across the Embassy lawn

Working the graveyard shift in Babylon
And the palm fronds are still, the evening's calm

And in a way it seems to me
There's nowhere else I'd rather be

Then watching the moonlight leaf
through the palm leaves

And come whatever may
I keep at my familiar ways

And I know it's for her love as much as the pay
That I'll play out the rest of my mercenary days

A Thousand and One Nights

"Dinarzade, having awakened about an hour before day, did what her sister had ordered her. 'My dear [Scheherazade],' she said, 'if you are not asleep, I entreat you, as it will soon be light, to relate to me one of those delightful tales you know. It will, alas, be the last time I shall receive that pleasure.'"
—*The Arabian Nights Entertainments, Middle East circa 9th century AD*
Scott Translation

Last night I dreamed
Scheherazade, it seemed
Whispered to me in the dark

And masterful her art
And the stars white and stark
And her voice warm and rich as the night

We journeyed past the sights
And the towering heights
Of the ziggurats and temples of old

And the treasures of gold
And the legends she told
Of this land's secrecies

And those mysteries, there that she breathed to me
The soaring majesties . . . now none to see
Sand stirring an empty sea

Sand
The wastelands
The once majestic land
Now I'm back again
Here where it all began

Walking through her enchanted nights again

Walking from the deserts of Anbar
To here beneath the headless scimitars
Arching over the blackness gleaming

And beyond the oil fires leaping
Surging into the night receiving
A perpetual Roman candle ablaze

And keeping the time over my race
The Cheshire clock face
The eternal watch ticking

And time like water dripping
Swelling, detaching and softly slipping
Into the instant's moment hanging

And, reflecting, refracting, rearranging
The carnival lights of the bridge railings
Falling over the side to the river whispering by

Soft like a sigh

Like the wind through the palm leaves, the desert trees
Murmuring, the evening breeze
Curls and twines like smoke serpentine

And winding into the warm night
The two rivers unite
The gray becomes the black

And we watch it all flow by
She and I tonight
The keepers of the flame

And I'm just another sentry without a name
Guarding an outpost in this antique domain

And like the other guards without faces
I'm one with the spirits that haunt these spaces

Staring down the moonlit promenade
One with the ghosts like Scheherazade

Ambien

"O God, I could be bounded in a nutshell and count myself a king of infinite space, were it not that I have bad dreams."
—William Shakespeare, Hamlet

where are you, my friend?
now I'm back again
back to the land of sand
these trips, they never end

hide and seek with the sun
and I've just begun
writing it all out in my journal
we were never meant to be nocturnal

I need you more than ever now
to quiet that dinning sound
and to gently unlock
the bands on my heart
and unwind
that knot in my mind
fiber by fiber
and all the reminders
the stresses, the pain
the doubts that remain
the silent refrain
that plays in my brain

then let it all slip
like a soft, gentle kiss
that complete release
and the soul-balming peace

and let me float free
like the wind on the sea
on my music that carries me
let it soar, let it bury me

but I lie here tonight
my brain forming stalactites
from the hours dripping by
glacial drops in my mind

my music to keep my sanity
to comfort me, carry me
riding high
on these my lullabies

watching the hours tick by

riding that desert plain
the same songs, again and again
those familiar strains

trying to add some sanctity, some gravitas
to all those countless hours I've lost
watching them hang
before they drop
piling on my back porch like so many dead leaves
would that I could grant just one reprieve

and I think my house is becoming haunted now

and I'm trying to compose one last requiem
before the wind scatters all of them
a final pavane
to play, lingering, at dawn

so I labor resolutely through the night
to build a monument to the dead hours of my life

look at my castle of sand
isn't it grand?

my castle is looking haunted now

that's not the only bat-filled belfry it seems
those are the same bats that are haunting my dreams

there must be some mistake
I can see my dreams when I'm awake

I sleep during the day
but these nights I can't go out and play
no more chasing shadows through
green and black
dreamscapes
now I just lie here awake

and the only shadows I chase now instead
are the phantoms of sleep fluttering over my bed

like so many bats

and later I'll put on my clown suit
and cavort in the light of the moon
mad as a loon

clowns are the only people with jobs now these days
but we'll always need our jesters anyways

jesters and satirists
to interpret all of this
and laughing, raucously bringing
some sense to the nonsense we all are living

aloof in our court of illusions
who are we fooling?
as the people tear each other apart
outside of our ramparts

and night is the new day
and the dogs will have their day

and the jester clowns gather round
out on the palace grounds
and toast!
with the bats and the ghosts
and the heavenly hosts!
and fall to laughing and mourning
as we wait for the morning

which is also the night
and I've lain up all "night"
with the bats and the clowns
might as well write it all down
turn that smile into a frown

as I lie alone in my bed
counting the clowns in my head
over and over and over again
wishing I had some fucking Ambien

Pilgrims

*"We are the Pilgrims, master; we shall go
Always a little further; it may be
Beyond that last blue mountain barred with snow
Across that angry or that glimmering sea."*
—*James Elroy Flecker*
*Hassan: The Story of Hassan of Baghdad and
How He Came to Make the Golden Journey to Samarkand*

The minaret squawks to life
during my inverted night
as I resolutely try to sleep
through the day
across the way
the wail drifting through the dawn air
calling the faithful there
to gather there
and begin their approach
their reverent approach
into the presence of God

The dawn prayer
the break of dawn
Al Fijr
sounds like
Infijar
explosion

And approaching
the Martyr, *Shaheed*, "witness"
has too prepared for this
dressed in white, bathed and shaven
he eases his explosive-laden
sedan towards the square
and slowly reverently there
the sojourners unite
and in the ignition
complete their submission

I note their transcendence vaguely
as an inconsequential *thud* faintly
drowning underneath the sounds
of the love-making emanating
from the screen in the room next door
and the actress's strident wailing
is slowly replacing
the sirens' noise-making
outside of our walls

And her urgent calls chronicle
another journey mystical
through the various stages
building, heightening, and wonderingly arriving
in that state liminal
just before the approach
that agonizing approach
into the presence of God

Today I just lie quietly here
trying to keep my head clear while outside
the various pilgrims are on their journeys
I'm in no hurry

I reach for my music again
as for an old familiar friend
and when I'm ready to move on
I'll switch to Warren Zevon
the right mixture of harmony and irony
anointed in prosody

A fitting soundtrack to my little spacewalk
suspended over the human condition

with the percussion punctuated by small arms
and the bombs bringing in the bass riff

Then I can howl down the moon
with the werewolves, rebels and desperadoes
before reflecting on those
departed before us
and then ascending in the cathartic chorus
in that instant's culmination
a simultaneous lamentation and celebration

As the pilgrim finally comes home
and bearing witness to the dreams lost and the stars crossed
the triumphs and the tragedies that
comprise the wonder of it all
with fear and trembling and awe
can enter the presence of God

Tigris

*"[The god Marduk] created the beasts of the field
and the living creatures of the dry land.
Tigris and Euphrates he formed,
and set them in their places,
and gave them good names."*
—A Second Babylonian Account of the Creation
Mesopotamia, circa 2nd Millennium BC
Muss-Arnolt translation.

dark and mysterious
the Tigris flows down her centuries
rippling against her shadowy shores

she has witnessed it all
armies of corpses she has swallowed
bearing her burdens to eternity

wishes cast like fishnets
the dreams that have been made on her banks
the reflections of stars in the water

harvests along her shores
the promise of life in the desert
along with the certainty of death

and she bears the rest away
through her silkily, slipping water
through the timeless silt of her banks

Babylon rose and fell
the gods had their towers and their glories
Ishtar's gate is no more but the river endures

and in the lapping on her shore
is she laughing or crying at the
human tapestry she is weaving by

or maybe she is just
whispering in the wind in the marsh grass
before she passes on her way

bearing her secrets within her breast
and forever laying them to rest

The Thieves of Baghdad

*"And he cried, A lion: My lord, I stand continually
upon the watchtower in the daytime,
and I am set in my ward whole nights:
And, behold, here cometh a chariot of men,
with a couple of horsemen.
And he answered and said, Babylon is fallen, is fallen . . ."*
—King James Bible, Isaiah 21:8-9

writing poems out in the desert again
searching the truck for a lousy, goddamned pen

one desert voice slowly babbling itself hoarse

wandering aimlessly in this place
my hair and beard growing over my face
crying to the winds and the sand
echoing over the rocks, the rocks of this wasteland

but if a tree falls in the forest does it make a lonely chorus?

and I'm alone here, one with the moon
grooving to my own internal tune
cat and mousing with the sun, sleeping by day
who does a graveyard shift in a graveyard anyway?

and outside of the palisades
are the sepulchers from that other crusade
all the beautiful mansions on display
empty as the dreams from that charade

and I'm just here, the vagabond satirical
wandering through this junkyard of poetic material
trying to drudge
some inspiration from the river's sludge

and the stench of the city's bowels in the toxic cloud most foul
that I watch forming over the skyline each morning
piecing through the broken metaphors
in the bombed out villas along the shore

keeping time
logging time
killing time

trying to make just one lousy rhyme out of this absence of reason
this is an absurdly surreal season

and we're all prisoners of our design, marking time
behind the concrete walls and concertina lines
watchtowers and minarets vying to dominate the view
reminds me of a Dylan tune

I guess I'm the Joker even if I still have a few beliefs
but where in the world is my good friend the Thief?

and who is the real Thief of Baghdad these days?
Ali Baba has long since been on his way
or was it Sinbad or maybe still another?
Doug Fairbanks stealing the Caliph's daughter?

I'm getting my myths all mixed up now
so busy writing my own down

we're all Thieves of Baghdad, don't you know?
from the first Forty to the Mongols to Sykes and Picot
taking our turns with you over the years
but you're the one who's the whore, Babel, my dear

cause even though we've fucked you all through the centuries
we've never gotten to the heart of your mysteries
and you take something more out of us each time
we always leave some part of ourselves behind

and I'm here at the last castle, manning the ramparts
guess you had the last word, you dirty old harlot
cause neither our money nor our lives will ever suffice
you can break our hearts, but we must ever pay your price

Eid-al-Fitr, Baghdad, 2013

> *"As flies to wanton boys are we to the gods;*
> *they kill us for their sport."*
> —William Shakespeare, *King Lear*

The Shia shoe shop owner, shell-shocked
told the AP: "I could hardly see
because of the smoke.
We had a terrible day that was supposed to be nice."

And I don't know whether to laugh or cry
as I watch these people die

On the roof of the Embassy
I can see the new amusement park
where mothers in hijabs
ride the Ferris wheel
and the children squeal

Carnival lights on the rides
lighting the night
like the flares shooting up over the river
and the wails of the sirens linger
over this balmy evening

60 people were blown up today
Happy Eid, everybody
Eid Sayyid . . .

And did you notice that if you rearranged "Eid"
it spells "IED?"
and there goes another one
this day is not yet done

And what do you think the gods make of this?
the antics of the ants, doing their little dance
trying to make themselves laugh or at least just smile
in the while of the hour
they have before they are devoured by the rest

And the wheel turns
and the mothers and children
ascend for a moment over the lights and the strife
and briefly behold the night
the cityscape's silhouettes
the minarets
for an instant, magnificent
before their little baskets descend
and it all continues again
with the sirens chanting below us
like some tragic Greek chorus
round and round the wheel
4000 Iraqis dead this year

round and round
round and round they go

Event Horizon

*"... how can you imagine what particular region
of the first ages a man's untrammeled feet may take him
into by the way of solitude—utter solitude ...
by the way of silence, utter silence ..."*
—Joseph Conrad, Heart of Darkness

the interesting thing about confinement
is that it leads to a certain refinement

of thoughts and reflections
as you sit in solitary introspection

bouncing thoughts like

                ping pong balls

off the walls in your trailer
and here

                you are

a little subatomic particle

                in orbit

from your room

                to the gym

chow hall

                            then duty shift

but does this make you

                            a strange

quark
or a charmed

                            quark?

working in the

                            liminal

stages between
the dawn and the

                            dark

nocturnal
diurnal
continuing in an infernal circle

                            of days

my tablet computer my

                            portal

to the outside world
and a funhouse mirror
within my interior

                                      maze

delving into the shelves

                                      of the seers

Dylan Thomas and Shakespeare

                                      my dear

friend Stephen King
and

                                      lately

Stephen Hawking

                                      digging

into theoretical physics
trying to become my own

                                      mystic

so, Dr. Hawking, riddle me this
you claim a witness from a distance
would perceive time slow
at the boundary of a dead star
I would counterpose
that we needn't travel so far

I can find deviations in the space-time continuum
here in the remnants of this once great civilization

as I gaze at my own event horizon-line
increasingly defined by
Baghdad city skylines and guard towers

the marching of the hours
marked by the minaret calls
then, as darkness falls
I sense the approaching pause

and from afar, I see
as through a glass, and darkly
myself at that last perimeter
before collapsing toward the center
of my own
black hole
and time
slows

        and

                then

                        stops

My Box

*"So I my
thoughts must,
oft miserable,
from country separated,
far from my friends,
in fetters bind . . ."*
—*The Wanderer, Britain
circa 10th century AD
Thorpe Translation*

This is my box
and I carry it with me wherever I go

I can do this because it is so compact
It can fit in a suitcase, assault pack or rucksack

I can put it in a pallet on a C-17
or under the seat in front of me

Above in the overhead storage
or below in the luggage hold

I take it on every deployment
because its assembly takes only a moment

Set it up in my room, or pod, or hooch
and even if I'm living with twenty dudes

I always have my privacy
there where no eyes can see

me in space
my private place

Alone in my box
just me and my thoughts
there on the FOB
boxes
within boxes
within
sandboxes

And after working all day or all night
I can pull it out and climb inside

And I'll decorate the walls with pictures and tapestries
some real memories
some idealized fantasies
some nice quotes
snatches of poetry
probably some pornography
all the different pieces of me

And there will always be music

And I'll be alone in this my home
and nothing can reach me inside my box
see into my space, past the locks

And nothing can hurt
not stresses from work
or drama from the States
or the ache of living
in this far-flung place
exiled from the rest of my race
as I orbit here out in outer space

For this is my home
and I take it with me wherever I go
tortoise-like on my back
winding the fateful track

And I exist
in this, my armor
my familiar
year after year
living it out inside of here

And then I return home
but I am not home
because my home is my box
and I am in my box
and though I hear knocks
the voices of my family and friends
are muffled and broken outside my walls

Church

"Hear the tolling of the bells—Iron Bells!"
—Edgar Allan Poe
"The Bells"

there is no God here
only the demons we choose to exorcise
here before the Iron Altar
and cacophonous is our choir

Sepultura, Disturbed, Rammstein, Korn
Slayer, Pantera, Manson, and Gwar

Killswitch Engage, System of a Down, and Tool
like having your central nervous system scrubbed down
with steel wool

a thousand devils cackling in their hells
and the clanging iron banging like bells

chalk clouds rising like incense
as I do my penance
working toward my infernal reward
wrestling with my chains
like Laocoon with his snakes

barbell on my back, lunging
bellicose across the floor
my own Via Dolorosa
leading to my personal Golgotha

crucifixions in the squat rack
then continuing the attack
legs, back, core
more, then more plates on the bar
going for that knockout
the dizzying, vision-blurring lockout
and in that trembling release
receiving that peace
by shouldering this burden
we may put a heavier one down
and, puking, prostrate
we attain a temporary expiation
a fleeting reprieve

and it is in this way
that we may live to lift another day

Another Love Song

"Lying asleep between the strokes of night
I saw my love lean over my sad bed . . ."
—Algernon Charles Swinburne
"Love and Sleep"

The porn star's perfectly made-up face is seraphic
her smile enigmatic
On her knees ready to receive her benediction
from the other standing above her
The moment of anointment approaches, but I close this video
I'm already good to go

Mission complete
Transmission has ceased
As I discard the tissue with my issue, I wonder how much hand lotion
I've used over the course of ten deployments
Probably a small ocean

All these trips lead one to become relatively relativistic
As we seek to assuage our needs, we start to see
our actual sexual consummations as merely extensions
of all these solitary simulations

We bridge the physical lacunae
only to come to find
that the bridges to the mind are far more
tenebrous

For who is to say what is on my mind
as I lie intertwined in my girl's arms
Maybe it's the same scene I just watched in this
KBR trailer park
Maybe the harder we try to revert to life at home
the more we find ourselves alone
still out in the desert

Cross that oceanic divide only to find
you're still making love in your mind

Make enough trips
and you're perennially in a long-distance relationship
even when you're reunited
you're still alone somewhere inside

And still looking for some other excitement

The excitement that only comes with violence
Maybe that's what we really get off on
Just as the machine gun's song
brings its own release
a temporary peace in the mindlessness
The ecstasy of leaving bodies outside broken homes
comes with its own afterglow, don't you know?
Sex and Violence
The Babylonians had it right
The Queen of the Night
both of her delights one and the same
and once you've passed through Ishtar's gate, there is no escape
she'll consume your fate

Bringing you here today
going on eight years coming to this place
still trying to live the chase
Maybe one of those idiots outside will do something stupid
Maybe the gun at your side, you'll finally get to use it

Find that rush and release again
in the meantime, you're in your trailer watching pornos again

And stepping outside of your cell
you try to look beyond yourself
Making your way up to the roof
at least up here you have a view

The Tigris is there
and you stare at her

past the concrete towers and the T-wall barriers

And in your mind's eye
you walk down to the riverside
and bury your face in her dark clothes
try to cleanse what's left of your soul

And then giving in to her embrace
surrendering to her kiss
you slip softly beneath the surface

And wrapped in her love
she'll carry you down to the *Shatt-al-Arab*

And there you can finally be free
as she gently bequeaths you to the sea

These People

*"Well, you know, that was the worst of it—
this suspicion of their not being inhuman.
It would come slowly to one.
They howled, and leaped, and spun, and made horrid faces;
but what thrilled you was just the thought of
their humanity—like yours—the thought of
your remote kinship with this wild and passionate uproar."*
—Joseph Conrad, Heart of Darkness

These people . . .

My armored SUV moves through the sea of humanity
clogging these city streets

Ninjas in blue burkhas entreating at cars
begging for alms
their drugged babies dangling in their arms

Like faceless mimes playing charades
putting on the most piteous display of misery
they can possibly portray

Behind the protection of the bulletproof glass
and my expensive sunglasses
I look past them up the street

to where the club-footed kids
play on half-feet

and the double amputee weaves through traffic
on his little butt-skateboard

as kids implore to smear a dirty rag
across your windshield for a dollar

A little farther up the road
some little snot-nose
is pedaling industriously on his bicycle
as if leading the pack in an invisible race
a ridiculous smile lighting his face

He's an impoverished 10-year-old
living in a giant shit hole
where he can look ahead to a short and miserable life
but he's just so damn happy to be pedaling his bike

Or maybe he just stole it, the little fucker

These people . . .

Little schoolgirls in white headscarves
walking arm in arm
without the least bit of care
about how their future will be curtailed

when the Taliban come back in town
and start cracking back down
just give them a couple of years
after the U.S. pulls out of here

And those girls can look forward to a future of servitude
and getting jailed when they get raped
or for trying to escape
or getting acid thrown in their faces
if they don't keep in their places

And then they can turn into the walking blue tents
that pose and soundlessly lament
at the fate they couldn't escape
standing there in the quagmire
of the Kabul evening rush hour

drugged babies in their arms
soundlessly begging for alms

Stay in school, kids
don't do drugs

These people . . .

And maybe the most pathetic thing I ever saw
wasn't that bloody infant or the grenaded grandma

Years ago, outside a house near Mazar
I pulled security out in the courtyard
and listened to the consumptive coughing of the kids inside
and by my feet, overturned on its side
was the saddest, broken tricycle

And in traffic today, I watch that kid on his bicycle
pedaling his way up the street
as fast as he can pump his dirty feet

Maybe he'll crest the hill by the old British fort
and look out over the city to the north
and think of a world with a little more hope

a place where the air is clean
and it's okay to dream
and you can drink the water
and people respect one another

Or maybe he'll just get run over by one of these idiot drivers
and end up in a pile
a broken bike by the heaps of litter

Probably the best thing that could happen to him
all things considered

Of Electricity and Other Mysteries

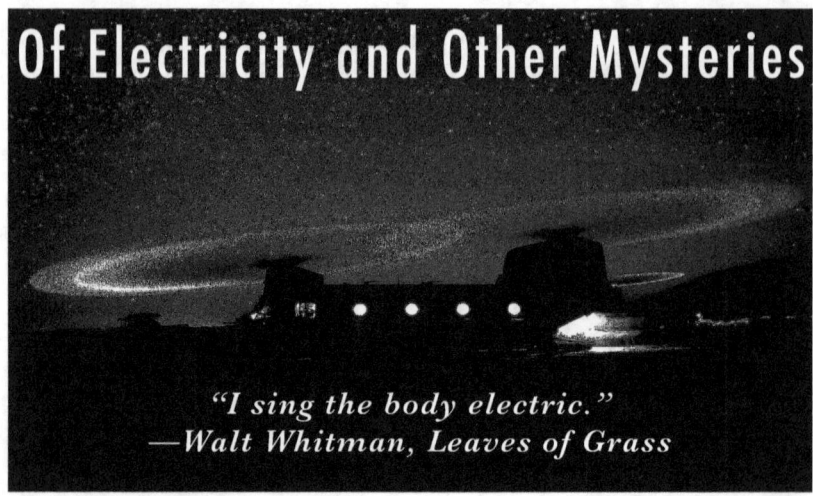

"*I sing the body electric.*"
—*Walt Whitman, Leaves of Grass*

our chemicals
chimerical
comprise our existence
in instants of emissions
electrical transmissions
synaptic firings like fireflies shining
in a fibrous web woven
by midnight spinners
Weird Sisters
glowing and gleaming
sparking and igniting

like scintillations from foundry machinery
or the arc of a welder's torch
or immolations in a porch bug lamp
winged messengers fried at two thousand volts
singing their last note on a millisecond death row
luminous ascensions like a log's leave-takings
flying up a flue
or distant glowings like marsh fires reflecting
in poisonous poolings
or enraged red as angered embers
blown by a bellicose bellows
or other-worldly like electric haloes forming
around rotor blades churning through the sandy night
fire-forged in strife

the roars, the rushes, the loves, the hushes
existent in a self-consuming instant

and the price we pay for these
ephemeral firings
selling your life away in the Middle East
whiling the time away for the pay and the hope
of another endorphin chain-reaction
firing like a 5.56 belt
rushing into a gun's hungry breach
burning, then fading into the sky
like tracer rounds reaching through the night
or lost, looking for the floating and then the drowning
in the flowing from the mouth of a bottle
the bar beckoning with a panoply of glass fingers
the liquid lurking in the low light
gleaming with a silent, heavy expectancy
promising lethe, nepenthe

or in the voodoo rattle of a prescription pill bottle:

promises, promises
pop this, pop this

step right up, step right up
this'll pick you up
yessir, yessir
that's not hissing you hear
no snake oil sold here!
lookee, lookee, nothing up this sleeve
this'll grant you your reprieve

take two with water
costs a dollar
but for you
I'll sell it to ya for four bits
you can't pass up this

I promise this
promise this

we must pick our potions sagely in this
Olde-Thyme Emporium
Whether it's a golly-gee ice cream and sodey-pop float
or one of the darker specimens floating
in jars behind the counter
we must craft our concoctions carefully, to be sure
mixing the distilments, elixirs, unctions, and tinctures

designing the lightning we are going to be riding

else we become that pile of rags and smells
holding a sign, "Veteran—Please Help"
or wrapped in a car's broken, metal embrace
and bloody kiss
dreams and promises racing through our veins

promises, promises
I promise this, promise this

trying to describe our lives in the space
between the flash and the thunder's crash

fireflies entangled and consumed
in a web of our own spinning
trapped and blinking
out our last beats

as we bleed out in the wreckage heap
or pass out in soiled bed sheets
or hang our heads alone to weep
or burn in a high-altitude freefall
because, Icarus-like, we tried to touch the sun
or in a vehicle fire in some foreign place
because, moth-like, we drifted too close to the flame

we must choose our combustions carefully

as our lighting bug lamps
and blazing oil fires
burn out in the night

overhead, the stars are constant in their cold-clear light

Bearing Witness

"Enough the light mysterious in the tree . . ."
—*James Elroy Flecker*
"I Rose From Dreamless Hours"

As I lie in the stillness
I reflect the closest I've come to fulfillment
is in the bearing witness

Bearing witness to the wonder

To the instant's mesmerization
to the gods of creation
and destruction

Watching the falling white stars through the green sky
darting like fireflies
and the soil of the earth resounding
to that distinctive buzzsaw sounding

Watching a white comet shoot to the earth below
with the sound of ripping Velcro

Watching multi-million dollar mechanical hornets
disintegrate a mud nest
Blackhawks gliding through the sky
like predatory fish, dark and streamlined

Witness to the fear
Witness to the awe
Witness to the wonder

Bearing witness to the beauty

I came across a hidden mountain lake near the top of the world
and never saw water so pure

I watched curtains of rain in all their serenity
flow through canopies of verdant greenery

I saw the moon hanging low in a lavender-slate sky
the light was fleeting and sublime

Bearing witness to the quiet wonder
Bearing witness to the loud wonder

Joyous wonder
Beethoven's Sixth
pastoral-bucolic barreling out of control into the Third Movement.

Soulful wonder
Van the Man bearing witness
fiery vision burning bright

A thousand other midnight carols,
lying awake floating through the playlist
out in some KBR oasis
spinning my iPod roulette wheel
coming out a winner each time
whiling away my time on my own private island
just another low man out looking for the promised land

Finding some solace in the wisdom of those before us
riding the chorus

And it's there in the poetry
as it was always meant to be

Itinerant, sojourner, pilgrim to some sacred space,
looking for that conduit
those few moments when time suspends
you transcend
God descends
and you can step outside yourself and simply experience
a silent witness
Hey, I lived this: I am here and Here is me
and it will be gone as I will be gone
in the moments, passing, fleeting

Like the shooting stars through the green-black night
writing out destinies with lasers burning white

And it was enough, I was here, I witnessed
Beethoven's Sixth
Fourth Movement into the Fifth

And now I can testify
I have seen the light, the day in the night

Leonard Cohen touching that secret chord
witnessing the here as well as the before

Dylan scribbling down his Back Pages in crimson flames
I have seen the light glowing through the refrain

Sunset impacting a rocky ridgeline
the desert on fire
a myriad of colors
a thousand different reds out to the horizon line

Maybe all you need in life
is a few such moments like this
maybe it is enough to say
I was here once, was, and witnessed

The Enemy

The eagle of his nest
No easier divest
And gain the sky,
Than mayest thou,

Except thyself may be
Thine enemy;
Captivity is consciousness,
So's liberty.
—Emily Dickinson, "Emancipation"

I've seen this movie before
watched it play out
as on a looping reel
everything so surreal
the green cityscapes in front of me
as I searched for my enemy

scanning my IR spotlight through the night
exploring the crevices and recesses that reach
into this spectral darkness
that stretches out through my sector of fire

reflecting off the eyeballs of the stray dogs
whose calls announce us this evening
a steady chorus of howling
our lights gleaming off their orbs
turning them into demons
that turn and run
turn and run away from me
as I search for my enemy

locking down the door of that Iraqi mud house
praying that he will come out and play tonight
and we can sort this out
make things right

but I don't see my enemy
he doesn't show his face to me
and 3rd Squad grabs the HVT
and everyone is RTB

and we fly back to the FOB
and I take my kit off
set it there in my cubbyhole
switch off my rifle optic's reticle
take a brush and knock the dust off
no need for a deep clean
I didn't fire a shot

fast-forward to the next night and the next
kicking down doors in someone else's mud nest
going through the villages, plains, draws and valleys
mountains and hilltops, looking for that enemy

Ramadi, Mosul, Al Anbar
Khost, Mez, and Kandahar

following the Euphrates
floundering through wadis
wading through the waterless seas
looking for that enemy

I thought I had him cornered a few times
and that he died inside
those caves we lit up
but maybe I just slipped up
because he always seemed to get away
leaving me to hunt him another day

from Colorado to Georgia
Denver to Atlanta
then I realized I was back in America

trying to find that face on which to focus my rage

and I found as much to hate back in the States
as I ever did in those foreign places

the civilians in their smiling insincerity
who came to be more vile to me
in their duplicity and shallowness
than the Others ever did

and so we keep on moving on
looking for the Others to transpose our hatred on
seeking out the world's conflict zones
looking for that threat you can call home

but the more we escape to other countries
the more we seem bound by our own baggage

and it came to me the other day
that there was only one enemy after all
disguised there in the siren's call

hidden in the cracks in the wall
that I count on the nights that I lie there awake
thoughts like snowflakes that won't subside
whirling in the globe of my mind

can't stop thinking about your own failures
they are written there in indelible ink
so you'll always remember

all the shortcomings and missteps
the fuckups and regrets
as much as you try
you're still running patrols in your mind's eye
still trying to find that battlefield where you can finally
prove yourself

well, if nothing else
a session at the gym, a good day at the range
that's enough to buy time for another day

and maybe that's all to which I can aspire
not a victory, maybe just a ceasefire
when you can come to terms with the reflection in front of you
then you can declare a truce
an armistice, from which to make some peace from this
and in that detente, you can finally lay down your arms
and embrace the person you are
and take some space from the absurdities of war
and just move on
on towards a new horizon

so, I'll wait for that day with its brighter dawn
but abide by hunting my ghosts in Babylon

Photo Credits
Part 1: Back To Babylon

Front Cover: Jeremy Rodriguez, Scoti Domeij

Part One: Back to Babylon: Illustration by Mark Reeve

Back to Babylon: Illustration by Mark Reeve

Al Anbar Nights: Combat Cameraman supporting the 75th Ranger Regiment

Jacking Off in the Port-O-John: Mikael Damkier (c) 123RF.com

Cannelure: Jonathan Baxter

The Assaulters: 1st photo: SPC. Justin A. Young; 2nd Photo: SPC. Christian Palermo, 75th Ranger Regiment Facebook page. URL: https://www.facebook.com/The-75th-Ranger-Regiment-190158030999896

When That Was Your War: Army Ranger Regiment Facebook page. U.S. Navy photo of WWII Rangers.

Ghosts of the Khyber: Illustration by Mark Reeve

Theories of Relativity: Army Ranger Regiment Facebook page. Photos by SPC. Steven Hitchcock.

The Night the Giant Robots Came: Army Ranger Regiment Facebook Page

The Jester Skull: Jeffrey Thompson (c) 123RF.com

Ghost Halls: Unattributed U.S.A.F. photo. URL: commons.wikimedia.org

A Love Like a War Zone: Army Ranger Regiment Facebook Page

//*NOTHING FOLLOWS:* Jonathan Baxter
Moving Out, Moving On: 1st photo: SGT. Brian A. Kohl. 2nd photo: Unattributed. Both photos from 75th Ranger Regiment Facebook page.
Racetracks: 75th Ranger Regiment Facebook Page

Part 2: Mercenary Days

Part Two: Mercenary Days: Illustration by Mark Reeve
Ambien: nomadsoul1 (c) 123RF.com
Pilgrims: Jonathan Baxter
Tigris: Jonathan Baxter
The Thieves of Baghdad: Wikimedia Commons photo by USAF MSgt. Michael E. Best.
Eid-al-Fitr, Baghdad, 2013: Wikimedia Commons photo by U.S.N. photographer PO2 Eli J. Medillin.
Event Horizon: Library of Congress photo from Wikimedia Commons.
My Box: Jonathan Baxter
Church: Jonathan Baxter
These People: 1st photo: U.S. Army photo by SSG. Andrew Smith. 2nd photo: U.S. Army photo by SSG. Lasonya Morales. Photos from Wikimedia Commons.
Of Electricity and Other Mysteries: U.S. Army photo by SGT. Michael J. MacLeod. Photo from Wikimedia Commons.
Bearing Witness: Combat cameraman attached to the 75th Ranger Regiment.
The Enemy: Combat Cameraman attached to the 75th Ranger Regiment.

Appendix 1: Recommended Resources

"The future is meant for those who are willing to let go of the worst parts of the past."—Corey Taylor

The organizations below offer both resources and referrals to other organizations that address the total picture of the interconnected issues you may face.

The Warrior's Journey: www.thewarriorsjourney.org

Warriors hold to a set of guiding principles that shape their worldview and characterize their community. Each branch of service offers its own focus, but all hold to core truths about the value of defending the constitution and honoring the legacy of those who served before them. The Warrior's Journey is an online resource for the military community offering trusted content relating to the mission, vision, challenges, and ethos of the warrior. Offering insight, perspective, and support, The Warrior's Journey empowers and equips warriors and their families to find wholeness in everyday life.

Are you contemplating suicide or experiencing a psychological health crisis?

GallantFew: www.gallantfew.org

GallantFew, Inc. coaches, mentors and networks veterans to help them transition to civilian lives filled with hope and purpose. Founded by veterans to veterans, GallantFew's mission is to prevent veteran isolation by connecting new veterans with hometown veteran mentors, thereby facilitating a peaceful, successful transition from military service to a civilian life.

GallantFew does this by creating and supporting a nationwide network of successfully transitioned veterans who engage locally with new veterans with the same military background going through transition. To welcome, connect, and include new veterans, GallantFew motivates communities all over the nation to take responsibility for returning veterans.

GallantFew believes this will prevent veteran unemployment, homelessness and suicide.
If you need help, make the call. PLEASE DO NOT TAKE ACTION OF ANY SORT until you talk to:
Phone: Army veteran Karl Monger at 817-600-0514
Phone: Army veteran Clarence Matthews at 843-697-0739
Log online to email GallantFew: www.gallantfew.org/contact/
Facebook: www.facebook.com/gallantfew
Twitter: www.twitter.com/gallantfew
YouTube: www.youtube.com/user/GallantFewInc
Address: P.O. Box 1157, Roanoke, TX 76262

Do your demons stir and murmur deep?

Vets4Warriors: www.vets4warriors.com
Vets4WArriors provides 24/7 confidential, stigma-free peer support by veterans to active duty, National Guard and reserve service members, veterans, retirees, and their families and caregivers. All calls are confidential. No information is shared with military branches or units. You are never alone, a caring, empathic veteran or service member is ready to connect with you and follow up.
Vets4WArriors are available to service members and their families who do not want to engage in mental health counseling, as well as, those who currently receive counseling, but need additional support.
Phone: 855-838-8255 Toll Free, available 24 hours a day, 7 days a week for all service members in the U.S.
If serving outside the United States: Call the Global DSN Operator at: DSN 312-560-1110 (Be sure to dial as a DSN number only) or Commercial: 719-567-1110.
Email: Info@Vets4Warriors.com
Log online and chat: www.vets4warriors.com/about/contact.html
Facebook: https://www.facebook.com/Vets4Warriors

Team Red White and Blue
Team Red White and Blue creates quality relationships and experiences that contribute to life satisfaction and overall wellbeing that consists of three core components—health, people, and purpose—which define a rich life.
   Team Red White and Blue Team RWB members share more than just values. Team Red White and Blue shares an ethos—a set of guiding beliefs and ideals that characterize our community.

Passion: We care more, we work harder, and we share our story.
People: Veterans and community drive everything we do.
Positivity: We don't ignore the challenges, we just stay positive and attack them.
Commitment: We are dedicated to each other, our mission, and our communities.
Camaraderie: We improve lives through genuine, personal relationships.
Community: This is what we are building…at every level.
Log online to email Team Red White and Blue: www.teamrwb.org/contact-us
Check out a chapter near you: www.teamrwb.org/get-involved/join-the-team
Facebook: www.facebook.com/TeamRWB
Twitter: www.twitter.com/teamrwb
Flickr: www.flickr.com/photos/teamrwb/sets
YouTube: www.youtube.com/user/TeamRWB
Address: 1110 W. Platt St., Tampa, FL 33606

Are you struggling to find a purpose and a mission?

Team Rubicon: www.teamrubiconusa.org

Team Rubicon unites the skills and experiences of military veterans with first responders to rapidly deploy emergency response teams. Team Rubicon's primary mission provides disaster relief to those affected by natural disasters, be it domestic or international. By pairing the skills and experiences of military veterans with first responders, medical professionals, and technology solutions, Team Rubicon aims to provide the greatest service and impact possible.

Through continued service, Team Rubicon seeks to provide our veterans with three things they lose after leaving the military: a purpose, gained through disaster relief; community, built by serving with others; and self-worth, from recognizing the impact one individual can make.

Coupled with leadership development and other opportunities, Team Rubicon looks to help veterans transition from military to civilian life. The driving force behind all of Team Rubicon's operational activity is service above self. Our actions are characterized by the constant pursuit to prevent or alleviate human suffering and to restore human dignity—we help people on their worst days.

Phone: 310-640-8787
Log online to email Team Rubicon: www.teamrubiconusa.org/contact-us

Facebook: www.facebook.com/teamrubicon
Twitter: www.twitter.com/teamrubicon
Instagram: www.instagram.com/teamrubicon
Vimeo: www.vimeo.com/channels/teamrubicon
YouTube: www.youtube.com/user/teamrubiconusa
Google+: www.plus.google.com/+TeamrubiconusaOrg/posts
Address: National Headquarters, 6171 Century Blvd. Suite 310, Los Angeles, CA 90045

Do the deep wounds of war possess your mind?

The Tragedy Assistance Program for Survivors: www.taps.org

The Tragedy Assistance Program for Survivors (TAPS) offers compassionate care to all those grieving the death of a loved one who served in our Armed Forces. Since 1994, TAPS has provided comfort and hope 24 hours a day, seven days a week through a national peer support network and connection to grief resources, all at no cost to surviving families and loved ones. TAPS has assisted over 50,000 surviving family members, casualty officers, and caregivers.

TAPS serves ALL survivors: adult children, children, ex-spouses, extended family, friends and battle buddies, grandparents, parents, siblings, widows/widowers/widowed and significant others through survivor grief seminars, suicide survivor grief seminars, retreats, expeditions, 'inner warrior' events and an online community.

The TAPS Military and Veteran Caregiver Network provides pre- and post-9/11 era military and veteran caregivers with peer support and partners to reduce their isolation and increase their sense of connectedness, engagement, hopefulness, wellness and their knowledge and skills.

800 Phone Number: If you just need someone to talk to, please call TAPS any time at 1.800.959.TAPS (8277). The TAPS survivor care team can also tell you about services and programs you might find helpful. The TAPS resource and information helpline is available 24 hours a day, 7 days a week, 365 days a year.
Phone: 202-588-TAPS (8277) FAX: 571-385-2524
Facebook: www.facebook.com/TAPS4America
Twitter: www.twitter.com/TAPS4America
YouTube: www.youtube.com/supporttaps
Address: National Headquarters. 3033 Wilson Boulevard, Suite 630, Arlington, VA 22201

Is the bottom of the bottle numbing your inner war?

Transformations Treatment Center:
www.transformationstreatment.center

Transformations Treatment Center (TTC) is a primary substance abuse treatment center in Delray Beach, FL. Licensed and accredited by CARF and the Joint Commissions, TTC provides a continuum of care to include: inpatient detox, partial hospitalization, intensive inpatient and outpatient services. Depending upon the client's needs, TTC offers 12-step traditional and Christian dual diagnosis treatment programs lasting between 30 to 90 days. There are four treatment niches: adult, young adult, Christian and first responder/veteran.

TTC takes a holistic approach that not only treats the addiction, but also heals the mind, body and spirit—as well as the family, an important element often overlooked by other treatment centers. TTC offers excellent diagnostics, assessments, treatment planning and medical care to teach all clients how to maintain a lifestyle of recovery worth protecting to get their lives and relationships back on track. TTC takes most insurances. Anyone with Tri-Care can call the admissions number and TTC can refer you to a facility they trust.

Admissions Phone: 877-995-0944
Cell Phone: 561-628-4871
Fax: 561-819-0631
Email Contact: Admissions@transformationstreatment.com
Address: 14000 South Military Trail, Suite 202, Delray Beach Florida, 33484
Facebook: www.facebook.com/TransformationsTC
Twitter: www.twitter.com/ttcrecovery
Instagram: www.instagram.com/ttcrecovery

Recommended Reading List

The Other Side of Me: Memoirs of a Vietnam Marine, Jim Bob Swafford
The Inside Out Revolution, Michael Neill
Man's Search for Meaning, Viktor Frankl
Jesus Was an Airborne Ranger, John McDougall
A Warrior's Garden, Ralph Gaskin
Violence of Action: The Untold Stories of the 75th Ranger Regiment in the War on Terror, Marty Skovlund, Jr., LTC. Charles Faint, Leo Jenkins
On Assimilation: A Ranger's Return From War, Leo Jenkins
Boots to Loafers: Finding Your New True North, LTC John W Phillips
Steel Will: My Journey through Hell to Become the Man I Was Meant to Be, Shilo Harris and Robin Overby Cox
Ashley's War: The Untold Story of a Team of Women Soldiers on the Special Ops Battlefield, Gayle Tzemach Lemmon

Other Books from Blackside Publishing

A Soldier to Santiago: Finding Peace on the Warrior Path

Has life passed you by? And you fit in—nowhere?

*I gave the best years of my life to a cause—
to a belief that proved false.
I loved living on the edge.
The thrill of standing the watch.
Rushing into harm's way
on behalf of my country.
For over 22 years and with pride,
I represented America
by wearing the cloth of the nation.
When my service was all over?
Life had passed me by and . . .
I fit in — nowhere.*
SCPO Brad Genereux

Is forgiveness and peace within the grasp of those who spent their lives pursuing the next mission on behalf of their country? Brad Genereux traces two parallel journeys—one through the inferno of war in Afghanistan, and the other through the healing purgatory of the Camino de Santiago. Juxtaposed between a combat zone and The Way of Saint James, experience two adventures and the two lives of one man. Willing to sacrifice his life to aid the Afghanis, Brad's candid account chronicles the challenges to carry out missions while operating under a complex chain of command, Afghani corruption, and deadly sabotage by the Taliban.

After Genereux retired from the military, he faced the arduous pursuit to assimilate into civilian life and to make sense of the unexpected deaths of three family members. Brad revisits dark demons imprisoning his spirit and the peace and healing unlocked on The Way of Saint James. *A Soldier to Santiago: Finding Peace on the Warrior Path* shadows the reflections of a war-hardened man devoid of identity and purpose and his search for answers, hope, and himself on a 769-kilometer trek over the Pyrenees and across northern Spain.

Are you searching for purpose and peace? Experience the camaraderie of warriors deployed to the battlefield and the *esprit de corps* of Camino peregrinos as they triumph over the inner battles of the spirit. Are you suffering from isolation, hypervigilance, nightmares, or insomnia? Join Brad in the Spring or Fall on The Way to find peace on the warrior path. If you're interested in trekking the Santiago de Camino, contact Brad.
Email: bgenereux@mail.com
Facebook: www.facebook.com/brad.gener.1
Instagram: www.instagram.com/bradgenereux/
Author: Brad Genereux
Foreword: Heather A. Warfield, Ph.D.
Published: September, 2016
Available in both paperback and e-book.

Triumph Over Terror
Are you searching for comfort and wondering, "Where is God?" amidst terror and turmoil?

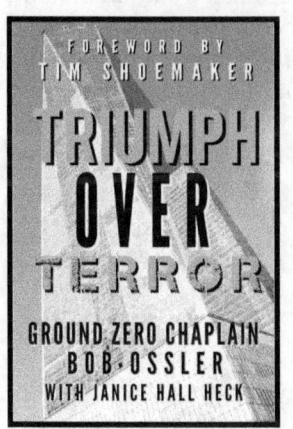

The day that changed the world—September 11, 2001—propelled America into the long war, the Global War on Terror. Like many Americans who serve our country, Chaplain Bob Ossler donned his firefighter turn-out gear, boarded a plane, and made his way to Manhattan and Ground Zero to help in any way possible. He was escorted onto the smoldering, quaking heap, dubbed "The Pile." Entering into the Gates of Hell—the crematorium and morgue for nearly 3000 beloved souls—an electrifying chill of horror shot through him.

Trained as a professional first responder, Ossler served five tours of duty during the cleanup at Ground Zero after 9/11. His eyewitness vignettes recount the questions, fears, struggles, and sacrifices of the families and workers overwhelmed by despair.

Chaplain Ossler conducted over 300 mini-memorials for the fragmentary remains carried off the Pile. He comforted the mourners, the frightened, and the heartbroken laborers sifting through millions of tons of carnage for the remains of their faith, their friends, and the unknown dead.

From the broken fragments of glass, steel, and men, Chaplain Ossler's mosaic of God's grace unveils the outpouring of generosity, heroism, and unity from people who stepped up to do "something." *Triumph Over Terror* honors the ultimate sacrifice and bravery of first responders who rush toward terror to save lives.

What do Ossler's insights reveal about finding meaning and purpose in the thick of chaos and personal tragedy? Chaplain Ossler chronicles the best of humanity—acts of courage and goodness in the midst of unimaginable devastation. As terrorist attacks continue to assault humanity, *Triumph Over Terror* reveals how your spirit can triumph over terror's reign and how you can help those suffering from trauma and loss.

No stranger to devastating tragedy, Bob Ossler, a Chicago firefighter and chaplain, was also on the scene to serve after Hurricane Katrina. In 2013, he also served the families of the 19 elite Granite Mountain Hotshot Firefighter Squad who perished in the Yarnell Hill Fire in Arizona.

Authors: Ground Zero Chaplain Bob Ossler with Janice Hall Heck
Foreword: Tim Shoemaker
Published: August, 2016
Available in both paperback and e-book.

Violence of Action: The Untold Stories of the 75th Ranger Regiment in the War on Terror

Violence of Action offers heartfelt, first-hand accounts from, and about, the men who lived, fought, and died for their country, their Regiment, and each other. Whether you served in the military or are a fan of military history or just want to know more about your fellow man in times of war—this is the book for you.

Authors: Marty Skovlund, Jr. with LTC Charles Faint and Leo Jenkins
Foreword: Mat Best
Published: October, 2014
Available in both hardcover and e-book.

www.ingramcontent.com/pod-product-compliance
Lightning Source LLC
Chambersburg PA
CBHW070146080526
44586CB00015B/1858